Orff We Go!

SEASONAL SONGS, GAMES AND
ORFF ACTIVITIES FOR THE MUSIC CLASS

By Cristi Cary Miller and Kathlyn Reynolds

T0068896

HAL•LEONARD®
CORPORATION
7777 W. BLUEMOUND RD. P.O. BOX 13819 MILWAUKEE, WI 53213

Visit Hal Leonard Online at
www.halleonard.com

Table of Contents

FOR LOWER GRADES

Autumn Wind 4
Bunny Boogie 6
Can You Move Like Me? 8
Diddle Dee Dye Dee Dee 9
Drum Game Song 11
Friendship Circle 13
Happy Valentine 15
Hey There! 17
Jack Be Nimble 18
A Lizard Named Claude 20
One of a Kind 22
Rhythm and Beat 24
See the Stars 25
Sing a Song of Solfege 27
Snowflakes 28
There's a Little Wheel a-Turnin' 30

FOR UPPER GRADES

Fairly Renaissance 32
Follow the Drinkin' Gourd 34
Fun wa ni alaafia 36
Jump Jive 38
Let Us Give Thanks 40
Let's Go to Mexico 42
Let's Take a Walk 44
Long May Your Colors Wave 46
Music Brings Us All Together 48
Music Makes Me Move 50
One Wintry Night 52
Pass the Rock 54
Pretty Little Miss 56
The Scene Is Halloween 58
Sleigh Ride 60
There's Magic in the Air 62

ORFF INSTRUMENT KEY

SG	Soprano Glockenspiel	AX	Alto Xylophone
SX	Soprano Xylophone	AM	Alto Metallophone
SM	Soprano Metallophone	BX	Bass Xylophone
AG	Alto Glockenspiel	BM	Bass Metallophone

ABOUT THE WRITERS

CRISTI MILLER is highly regarded across the United States as a master teacher, conductor and composer. After graduating from Oklahoma State University, she began her teaching career instructing grades 7-12. She eventually moved to the Putnam City School system in 1989 where she worked in the elementary classroom for 21 years. In 1992, Mrs. Miller was selected as the Putnam City Teacher of the Year and in 1998 received one of the four "Excellence in Education" awards given through the Putnam City Foundation. In 2008, she became a National Board Certified Teacher and in 2009, she was selected as the Putnam City PTA Teacher of the Year. Recently, Mrs. Miller became a part of the Fine Arts Staff at Heritage Hall Schools in the Oklahoma City area where she teaches middle school music. Cristi has served as the Elementary Representative on the Oklahoma Choral Directors Association Board of Directors as well as the Elementary Vice President for the Oklahoma Music Educators Association. She currently serves as the President for this organization. Along with her teaching responsibilities, Cristi authors and co-authors a column for a national music magazine entitled *Music Express* and was a contributing writer for the Macmillan McGraw-Hill music textbook series, *Spotlight on Music*. In addition, she serves as the consulting editor for Little Schoolhouse book series, *Christopher Kazoo and Bongo Boo*. Mrs. Miller is frequently in demand as a clinician and director across the United States and Canada with numerous choral pieces and books in publication through Hal Leonard Corporation. She has also been the recipient of several ASCAP awards for her music. Cristi and her husband, Rick, live in Oklahoma City.

KATHLYN REYNOLDS is a retired music educator with 30 years teaching experience in the Putnam City Schools. She is a frequent clinician/conductor at choral festivals and workshops throughout the southwest. Mrs. Reynolds was a co-director of the Putnam City Honor Chorus, an auditioned choir of 4th through 8th grade singers, for 10 years and headed the children's choir program at her church for many years. Currently, she co-authors a column for *Music Express!* a national music educators magazine, and is a contributing sacred music composer for the Hal Leonard Corporation. Mrs. Reynolds was honored as the Oklahoma Teacher of the Year in 1982 and has been recognized as a Director of Distinction by the Oklahoma Choral Directors Association and named to the Oklahoma Music Educators Hall of Fame. The National Retired Teachers Association presented Mrs. Reynolds the "With Our Youth" award for her service to children since retirement. Recently, she was a recipient of the "75 Who Made a Difference" from the University of Oklahoma's School of Education. Kathlyn and her husband, Bob, live in Oklahoma City and have two children, four grandchildren and one great grandchild.

Autumn Wind

By CRISTI CARY MILLER
and KATHLYN REYNOLDS

Voices: The wind!___ The wind!___ There blows the au-tumn wind. The

BM/BX: Think: "Wind, wind, au-tumn wind.

wind!___ The wind!___ There blows the au-tumn wind.

Wind, wind, au-tumn wind.

Whirl-ing and twirl-ing and spin-ning a-round. Danc-ing the leaves right off the ground.

Wind, wind, same, same wind.

Sing-ing a col-or-ful mes-sage so clear tell-ing the earth that au-tumn is here.

Wind, wind, same, same wind."

LESSON PLAN AUTUMN WIND

POEM TEACHING SUGGESTIONS

To prepare:
Create a visual of the poem shown here.

1. Present the poem visual:

> The **wind**! The **wind**! There blows the autumn **wind**.
> The **wind**! The **wind**! There blows the autumn **wind**.
> **Whirling** and **twirling** and **spinning** around,
> **Dancing** the leaves right off of the ground,
> **Singing** a colorful message so **clear**
> Telling the **earth** that autumn is **here**,
> The **wind**! The **wind**! There blows the autumn **wind**.
> The **wind**! The **wind**! There blows the autumn **wind**.

2. In rhythm, read the poem aloud to your students, using creative vocal expression.

3. Now have them read with you.

4. Ask students to recognize special words. Read together again, clapping on these words and practice all until secure.

5. Add suggested instruments to special words one at a time and perform.
wind = xylophone - glissando up
whirling = hand drum, finger tips circle edge
twirling = guiro
spinning = cabasa

dancing = tambourine
singing = resonator bells, "d" and "f" played together
clear = finger cymbals
earth = drum
here = woodblock

6. Internalize the poem using instruments only. (To help them feel the rhythm, point to the special words when they occur.)

7. Now, have students perform the poem aloud (with instruments) as you play the BM/BX accompaniment pattern on a keyboard or instrument.

MELODY TEACHING SUGGESTIONS

1. Sing the song for your students as you play the BM/BX pattern. Help them recognize ABA form.

2. Teach the A section by rote using four-measure phrases.

3. Teach the B section by using two-measure phrases; then four-measure phrases. Sing song until secure.

ORFF TEACHING SUGGESTIONS

1. Pat the entire BM/BX rhythm (ABA form) while speaking "think" words. (Move hands in A section to match the note pattern change.)

2. Lead students to discover the note/word differences between the A and B sections.

3. Have students join you performing the BM/BX part with "think" words. Transfer to instruments.

4. Snap the finger cymbal accompaniment as the BM/BX pattern is played. Transfer to instrument.

5. Demonstrate the AX/SX glissando on the instrument. Explain this part only happens in the A section. Transfer students to instruments.

6. Play in ensemble while singing the song.

> ***Movement Idea***
> *Space students randomly around the room and distribute colorful streamers/scarves to each one. During the A section, tell them to remain in place as they move their "colors in the wind." In the B section, allow them to travel around the room, "whirling and twirling and spinning around." Encourage good singing as they experience this movement idea.*

Bunny Boogie

By CRISTI CARY MILLER
and KATHLYN REYNOLDS

LESSON PLAN BUNNY BOOGIE

TEACHING SUGGESTIONS

1. Sing the song on "loo" as you hold fingers up to number each two-measure phrase. Ask students to identify like phrases.
2. Add words and sing again. Ask class to identify the rhyming words.
3. Teach m. 1 (with words) to the students. Have them echo until learned.
4. Ask students to sing the first measure of each phrase as you respond with the second measure.
5. Sing several times and switch roles. Finally, sing all of the song together.

ORFF TEACHING SUGGESTIONS

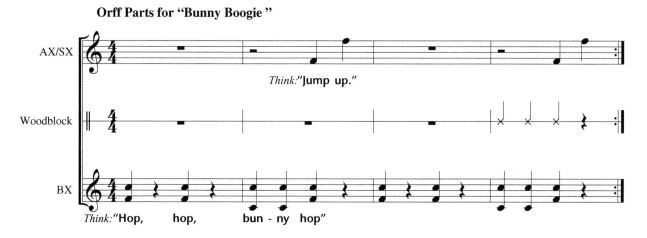

Orff Parts for "Bunny Boogie"

1. Have students pat the BX pattern while speaking the "think" words. (Move left hand to show melodic change.) Transfer to instruments. (For younger musicians, consider dividing ostinato between two students.)
2. Alternately snap the AX/SX part while speaking the "think" words. Transfer to instruments.
3. Clap the woodblock part. Transfer to instrument.
4. Sing the song as instruments play.

A "HOPPY" DANCE

Formation: *Concentric circles with partners facing each other*

Ms. 1-2   Partners join hands and alternately push/pull to the beat

M. 3   Release and flutter jazz hands at head level

M. 4   Alternately point down ("boogie woogie" style) on words

Ms. 5-6   Partners join hands and alternately push/pull to the beat

M. 7   Release and flutter jazz hands at head level

M. 8   With hands as bunny ears, hop three times to right (greeting new partner)

Can You Move Like Me?

By CRISTI CARY MILLER
and KATHLYN REYNOLDS

(Ma - ry, Ma - ry) walk - in' 'round the school. (She) gave me a high five be - cause I am so cool. She said: "Can you move like me? Can you move the way I do?" So I an-swered: "I can do it. I can do the same as you."

LESSON PLAN TEACHING SUGGESTIONS

1. Sing the song to the class as they pat a quarter note beat. Discuss with your students the two different parts to the song. (Singing/speaking, i.e. A/B)
2. Perform song again as students walk in place to the beat for the A section. For the B part, have them stop moving and clap their hands to the beat.
3. Ask students to echo song in two-measure phrases. Practice until learned.

GAME

Formation: *Standing circle with leader in the center*

1. Substitute in the name of the leader (for "Mary, Mary") as this person walks around the circle during the A section.
2. On the words "high five," this student stops and faces another player and gives them a "high five."
3. The leader then makes up a movement for "Can you move like me? Can you move the way I do?" (i.e. jump, clap, snap or any combination)
4. The player responds with the exact motions for "So I answered: 'I can do it! I can do the same as you.'"
5. The player then becomes the new leader. The game continues until all have had an opportunity to be in the center.

Orff Teaching Suggestions

1. Alternately pat the BX crossover pattern while speaking the "think" words. Transfer to instrument.
2. Practice playing the AM part in the air while speaking the "think" words. Move hands to show chord change. Transfer to instrument and play against the BX part.
3. Listen as you sing the song and snap the AG/SG part. Ask students to identify where these snaps occur (at the end of each phrase.) Now have them sing/snap with you. Transfer to instruments and play all three ostinati together.

For your younger students, *consider using this Orff accompaniment:*

Diddle Dee Dye Dee Dee

By CRISTI CARY MILLER
and KATHLYN REYNOLDS

LESSON PLAN TEACHING SUGGESTIONS

1. Sing the m. 1 motif on "loo" for the students and explain this melodic pattern is found throughout the song.
2. Sing the entire song on "loo" and challenge them to count how many times they hear the motif. (3)
3. Teach the words of the motif. Then, have students sing this part each time it occurs in the song as you respond with the other measures. Do this several times.
4. Discuss what happens melodically in ms. 5 & 6. (*It moves upward.*) Teach these measures and direct students to move their hands to show pitch direction.
5. Sing the song together, adding snaps and continue to practice until learned.

ORFF TEACHING SUGGESTIONS

1. Pat the BX part using alternate hands while speaking the "think" words.
   (Make certain to *mirror* this for the students.) Transfer to instrument.
2. Clap the AX pattern while speaking the "think" words. Transfer to instrument and play with the BX part.
3. Have the students sing the song with snaps as you play the AG/SG part. Ask them where this part occurs.
   (*On the snaps*) Transfer to instruments.
4. Add the hand drum/woodblock part to the words "use your eyes" and "use your ears."
5. Play in ensemble while singing the song.

GAME

To Prepare: *Find a favorite puppet to assist with this activity. In addition, write 8-10 (age appropriate) four-beat melodic patterns on separate pieces of paper. Present these as visuals.*

1. Use the puppet to guide the students to experience singing all the melodic patterns using solfege.
2. The game begins with the students performing the song. The puppet then sings one of the displayed patterns and the students are challenged to "use their eyes and ears" to discover the correct one.
3. Continue the game until all patterns have been identified.

Drum Game Song

By CRISTI CARY MILLER
and KATHLYN REYNOLDS

Lis-ten to the drum and walk the beat. Feel the pulse and put it in your feet.

Fol-low the di-rec-tions. Don't be slow. Drum game, fun game, here we go!

Drum Game Patterns

By CRISTI CARY MILLER
and KATHLYN REYNOLDS

Teacher:

(1) Walk eight beats and count out loud. Drum game, fun game, here we go!

Teacher:

(2) Walk sev-en beats and say "Hi!" on eight. Drum game, fun game, here we go!

Teacher:

(3) Walk eight beats and freeze eight beats. Drum game, fun game, here we go!

Teacher:

(4) Walk four beats stop and clap four beats. Drum game, fun game, here we go!

Teacher:

(5) Walk four beats and jump four beats. Then,
twist four beats and freeze four beats. Drum game, fun game, here we go!

LESSON PLAN DRUM GAME SONG

TEACHING SUGGESTIONS

Have students:

1. Start with a discussion of beat and where it can be found. (heart, clock, etc.)
   Explain that it can be put anywhere in their bodies.

2. Feel the beat as they respond with motions of clapping, patting, etc.

3. Pat their hearts as you sing the song.

4. Continue patting as they echo-sing this song in two-measure phrases.
   Repeat in four-measure phrases and sing until learned.

5. Walk around the room as you play a beat on the drum.
   Change tempos to improve listening and kinesthetic skills.

6. Walk and sing the song as you play the drum.

DRUM GAME

Have students:

1. Listen as you give instructions to the game. Give an example, "Walk eight beats
   and count out loud" means for students to walk around the room while counting to 8.
   Ask them to practice this pattern 4 times as you play a steady beat on the drum.

2. Experience all five patterns, as they count aloud.

3. Play the game in a rondo form as they sing the song and follow the spoken directions.

4. Play again as they count internally.

5. Extend this idea, using their imaginations to create new beat patterns.

ORFF SUGGESTIONS

Add a simple Orff ostinato to enhance the presentation.
(Two options are given.)

Option 1:

Option 2:

Friendship Circle

By CRISTI CARY MILLER
and KATHLYN REYNOLDS

Let's make a friend-ship cir - cle. Let's make a friend-ship cir - cle. Let's make a friend-ship cir - cle to meet and greet each one.

Say your name and when you do we will say it back to you.
(Sing) (sing)

My name is Mar - y. Her name is Mar - y.

Wood Block

Soloist: Class:

LESSON PLAN FRIENDSHIP CIRCLE

TEACHING SUGGESTIONS

1. As an introduction to this song, teach the following body percussion ostinato.

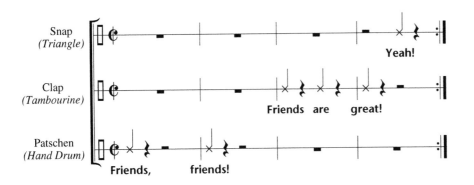

2. When the group is secure, have them perform the pattern while you speak the lyrics for the A section. Repeat this several times.

3. Sing the melody for the A section on "loo" and ask the children to identify like phrases. *(1 & 3)*

4. Add the words and have children echo-sing each 2-measure phrase. Challenge them to sing phrases 1 and 3 while you sing phrases 2 and 4. Switch parts and perform again. Sing together until secure.

5. Divide your class into two groups. Invite one half to perform the ostinato, selecting three students to accompany on suggested instruments, while the others sing the song. Exchange roles and perform again.

CIRCLE GAME

Formation: *Standing circle, one selected child ("greeter") with wood block*

1. Have the children sing the A section as the "greeter" walks around the inner circle.

2. At the end of this section, the greeter turns to the nearest student who will become the soloist. The greeter plays the wood block as the teacher/class chants the first four measures of the B section.

3. The soloist chosen will respond with their spoken or sung name.

4. The class repeats their response and the soloist takes the wood block and becomes the greeter that walks the inner circle.

5. The game continues until everyone has had a turn.

Happy Valentine

By CRISTI CARY MILLER
and KATHLYN REYNOLDS

hear my lit-tle plea.   If you'll be my Val-en-tine how   hap-py I will be!"

6

LESSON PLAN TEACHING SUGGESTIONS

To prepare: *Create a visual of the chart shown here.*

> Once there was a Valentine
> Who loved most everything.
> And when it met a brand new friend,
> Its' heart would start to sing,
> "Roses red, violets blue.
> Hear my little plea.
> If you'll be my Valentine,
> How happy I will be."

1. Rhythm speak the poem as students follow along.

2. Have the students join you in reading again.

3. Rhythm speak together several times as students clap on special words.

4. Have students repeat the above step but internalize the special words, continuing to clap.

5. Reverse the process and have students internalize the poem but continue to clap/speak special words.

6. Transfer the special words to the following instruments:
"Valentine" . . . . tambourine
"loved" . . . . finger cymbals
"friend" . . . . .cowbell
"sing". . . . . . . F#/D on tone chimes
"red" . . . . .wood block
"blue" . . . . .guiro
"happy" . . . . maracas

7. Use instruments on special words to accompany poem.

8. Teach melody.

9. Next, teach the body percussion ostinato (pat, clap, snap) while speaking "think" words. ("Hap-py Val-en-tine").

10. Divide students into two groups. Have one group perform the body percussion pattern as the other group sings the song. Switch roles and perform again. Finally, everyone sings with body percussion.

ORFF TEACHING SUGGESTIONS

Pat the xylophone pattern while speaking the "think" words. Include a snap at the end to denote the glockenspiel part. Transfer to instruments and play while singing.

Suggested Form

1. Speak poem with unpitched instruments

2. Pitched instruments perform introduction (Orff ostinato – two times)

3. Children sing song with Orff accompaniment

4. Interlude (Orff ostinato – two times)

5. Children sing song with Orff accompaniment and body percussion

6. Coda (Orff ostinato – two times)

Hey There!

By CRISTI CARY MILLER
and KATHLYN REYNOLDS

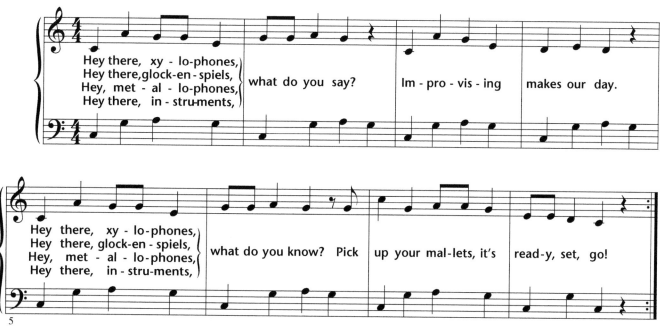

LESSON PLAN TEACHING SUGGESTIONS

1. To warm up, have students echo random patterns from a C pentatonic solfege ladder.

2. Next, lead them to echo/sing the melody in solfege one measure at a time, then in two-measure patterns and continue until song is learned.

3. Teach the words by rote and sing together as you play the bass pattern on a BX or keyboard.

4. When the song is secure, have students find a partner and teach the movement idea (see below).

5. Ask students to sing the first verse as they walk around the room, finding a new partner by the end of the verse.

6. Now have them perform the movement idea with partners while thinking that verse in their head. The movement is performed using the same music, instrumental only.

7. Place the three Orff families in groups and remove bars to make C pentatonic scales.

8. Select students to play the instruments and explain they will be improvising, or making up, a melody during the movement sections of the song. (B section)

Suggested Form

SING	Vs. 1 - Sing and walk
MOVE	Xylophones improvise w/partner movement
SING	Vs. 2 - Sing and walk
MOVE	Metallophones improvise w/partner movement
SING	Vs. 3 - Sing and walk
MOVE	Glockenspiels improvise w/ partner movement
SING	Vs. 4 - Sing and walk
MOVE	All instruments improvise w/partner movement

MOVEMENT IDEA

Formation: *Partners facing each other*

Ms. 1:	Pat, clap, partner clap, clap
Ms. 2:	Repeat above
Ms. 3:	Jump (making 1/4 turn to R), jump (making 1/4 turn to R), snap, snap
Ms. 4:	Repeat above
Ms. 5-8:	Repeat ms. 1-4

Jack Be Nimble

Words from Nursery Rhyme
Music by CRISTI CARY MILLER
and KATHLYN REYNOLDS

LESSON PLAN JACK BE NIMBLE

TEACHING SUGGESTIONS

A SECTION

1. Have students alternately tap their feet to a steady beat as you speak the nursery rhyme.

2. Tell them to echo the text by phrase, keeping the beat.

3. Continue process until poem is learned.

4. To teach the melody, have students echo as you sing and move by phrase. (Touch your shoulders for the "sol" pitch, head for "la," waist for "mi" and reach high for "do.") Sing until learned.

B SECTION

1. Ask students to perform this ostinato as you recite the poem. (Have them substitute patting the air for partner clap.)

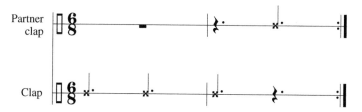

2. Again, echo the text by phrase, keeping ostinato, and continue until learned.

3. Have students find a partner. Practice ostinato together (replace with partner clap) while speaking the poem.

4. Practice again, encouraging one partner to speak Group I question, and the other Group II answer.

5. To reinforce their literacy skills, challenge the students to discover the rhyming words and the accompanying action (partner clap).

ORFF TEACHING SUGGESTIONS

1. Have students practice the above ostinato, transferring the claps to xylophones/metallophones and the partner clap to glockenspiels.

2. Play in ensemble while singing the A section.

MOVEMENT IDEA

Formation: *Two equal concentric circles (inside circle facing outside); Designate partners standing across from each other.*

1. For the A Section, have students sing and slide step CCW (counter clockwise) two phrases; then CW (clockwise) back to partners. (Circles will go in opposite directions.)

2. For the B section with partners facing each other, perform the movement ostinato as the outside circle recites Group I question and inside responds with Group II answer.

3. Teacher concludes by rhythm speaking these words:
Outside circle, let's begin.
Step to the right and we'll do it again.

4. Perform song again with new partners.

A Lizard Named Claude

By CRISTI CARY MILLER
and KATHLYN REYNOLDS

LESSON PLAN A LIZARD NAMED CLAUDE

TEACHING SUGGESTIONS

1. To introduce this limerick style, have your students echo clap two-measure 6/8 meter rhythms, using all levels of body percussion.

2. When students are comfortable with this meter, introduce the three ostinati that accompany the poem as one pattern. Add these suggested motions to go with the words:

Sssss = shake jazz hands
Go Claude = fist pump
He is a lizard who just loves to sing = tap index fingers together to the rhythm of the words

3. Challenge them to continue the ostinato as you **speak** the limerick to them.
(Do this several times.)

4. Teach the limerick having students echo speak one phrase at a time.
Continue this process until poem is secure.

5. Divide your class into two groups. One group will perform the limerick while the other speaks the ostinato. Switch roles and practice again.

6. Teach the limerick melody with the words, using the echo process as students move their hands to show pitch changes.
(Consider using Curwen hand signs.)

7. Add the limerick melody to the spoken ostinato.

INSTRUMENT TEACHING SUGGESTIONS

1. Divide your class into three groups and assign each one of the three ostinati.

2. Have them perform their parts with actions as you sing the limerick.

3. Transfer each ostinati to the suggested instruments and have them perform as the class sings the song.

4. Add this broken bordun pattern to accompany the poem:

One of a Kind

By CRISTI CARY MILLER
and KATHLYN REYNOLDS

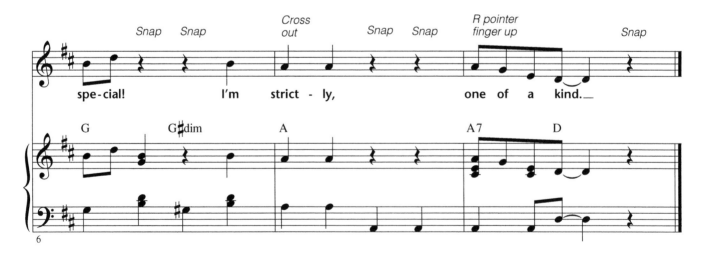

LESSON PLAN ONE OF A KIND

TEACHING SUGGESTIONS

1. Sing the song for your students, snapping on the quarter rests.
Then, sing again, having the students join you on the snaps.

2. Echo-sing with snaps in two-measure phrases and continue until song is learned.

3. Add choreography and sing again.

EXTENSION IDEA

To prepare: *Create strips of paper with four equal squares.*

1. Spend time letting your students discuss what makes a person unique and special.

2. Encourage students to name a trait they like about themselves, i.e. red hair, pretty smile, football player, etc. Write some of these ideas on the board.

3. Choose several characteristics and show students how to rhythm notate them within the squares. (Make certain they know each square represents one beat.) For example,

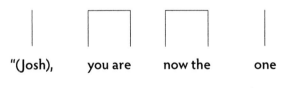

4. Now, select several more traits and have students discover the rhythm.

5. Give each student a rhythm strip and a pencil. Ask them to fill in the squares with something special about themselves and then have them notate the rhythm above the words. (For younger students, this task may require your help.)

6. Allow time for each student to practice his/her rhythm.

A "UNIQUE" PERFORMANCE IDEA

Formation: *Students sit holding their paper strips in their laps.*

1. Sing the song together with choreography.

2. At the conclusion, speak this chant to an individual student:

"(Josh),   you are   now the   one

(Josh) then holds up his rhythm and performs.

3. Repeat this line for three more students.

4. Sing the song again, continuing in a Rondo form until everyone has shared their rhythms.
Let this composition idea be a self-esteem builder as your students discover how "special" they are.

Rhythm and Beat

By CRISTI CARY MILLER
and KATHLYN REYNOLDS

LESSON PLAN TEACHING SUGGESTIONS

1. Have students echo clap/speak the words in two measure phrases, graduating to four-measure phrases. Add melody and repeat process.

2. When the song is learned, have students stand randomly around the room. Play a steady beat on a drum and ask them to sing as they walk the beat. Then explain, they have been walking to the beat of the music.

3. Ask students to clap the rhythm of the song while singing. (For young musicians, explain that the rhythm matches the words and demonstrate how it sounds before having them perform.)

4. When all parts are secure, ask students to walk the *rhythm* with you while singing.

5. To assess, play the *beat* or the *rhythm* of the song on a drum while singing. Have students identify which one they hear by raising one finger for beat or two fingers for rhythm.

6. Sing the song again with piano accompaniment.

DRUM CIRCLE GAME

Teacher sings: 1. Can you play this rhy - thm? *(Teacher claps rhythm)*
Students sing: 2. We can play this rhy - thm. *(Students echo on drums)*

Formation: *Seated circle*

1. Have students sing the song while patting a half-note beat.

2. Give drums to four students to begin the game.

3. Ask the class to sing again as the drums are passed around the circle to a half-note pattern.

4. When the song ends, the four students with instruments play the response to this melodic question. (We suggest two questions for each round.)

5. Play the game until all have had an opportunity to respond.

See the Stars

By CRISTI CARY MILLER
and KATHLYN REYNOLDS

LESSON PLAN SEE THE STARS

TEACHING SUGGESTIONS

1. Sing the song *a cappella* for the students and ask them to identify the rhyming words. As these words are discovered, write them on a board in sequential order. (You may need to perform the song several times.)

2. Sing the song again, but have the students fill in the *rhyming* words.

3. Finally, add the choreography as you have them echo sing with movement, one measure at a time. Expand to two measures and perform again.

4. Add the piano accompaniment and practice until the song and actions are learned.

RHYTHM READING ACTIVITY

To prepare: *Using craft paper, cut out six to eight large pentagrams (stars). On each, write a four-beat age appropriate rhythm. These rhythms should be large enough for the whole class to see and read.*

1. Review the rhythms with your students as they pat while speaking rhythm syllables. Practice these until secure.

2. Set out glockenspiels, removing bars to create a C pentatonic scale. (You may also substitute/add the following instruments: triangles, finger cymbals, tone chimes, resonator bells.)

3. Choose a "Star Catcher" to select a star rhythm for presentation, holding the star for all to see. (Option: Use two star rhythms for second and third grades.)

4. Next, select several students to perform the chosen rhythm(s) on the instruments.

5. Use the last two measures of the piano accompaniment as an introduction. Have the remaining children sing/move while the instrumentalists play the star rhythm as an ostinato to accompany the song.

6. Select a new "Star Catcher" – who chooses a new rhythm(s) – and add new instrumentalists. Continue activity until all have had an opportunity to participate.

Sing a Song of Solfege

**By CRISTI CARY MILLER
and KATHLYN REYNOLDS**

Sing a song of sol-fege, sim-ple as can be. Sing a song of sol-fege. Start with do re mi,

fa sol la ti do. Let sol-fege lead the way. Sing a song of sol-fege each and ev-'ry day.

LESSON PLAN TEACHING SUGGESTIONS

To prepare: *Create a visual of the song for each student.*

1. Review the solfege family names with your class. Use a solfege stepladder and invite students to echo-sing several patterns as you point to the pitches.
2. Next, focus on the pitches *sol, mi,* and *la* and have students echo-sing patterns using Curwen hand signs.
3. Teach the song by rote as students echo in two-measure phrases. Repeat using four-measure phrases and practice until learned.

ORFF ACCOMPANIMENT

Here are three patterns that may be used to accompany the song. Use the ostinato or combination that best fits your learners.

① *Think:* "Stead-y, stead-y. Keep it stead-y."

② *Think:* "Beat! Beat! Keep the beat!"

③ *Think:* "Cross-ing o-ver, Do Sol La Sol"

EXTENSION IDEA

1. Place your Orff instruments so that they are facing a board. Remove the bars to isolate *sol, mi* and *la.* (G, E, A)
2. Point out to your students how these bars represent solfege names/pitches.
3. Lead your students to echo sing and play various *sol, mi, la* patterns. (If you do not have enough instruments for everyone, make sure students take turns practicing this step.)
4. Draw two lines on a board. Label them in the following manner:
   La
   Sol ————————————
   Mi ————————————
5. Using iconic symbols, i.e. noteheads, create several four-beat *sol, mi, la* patterns on the lines (space) and have students sing with hand signs as you point to the pitches.
6. Next, have them repeat this process, playing the pitches on their instruments as they sing.
7. After this review, space your instruments out evenly. Assign part of the students to the instruments and place others evenly between.
8. Ask everyone to sing the song (with Orff accompaniment). While singing, choose one student to come to the board and create a four-beat *sol, mi, la* pattern.
9. When the song concludes, have those not playing, sing/hand sign the new pattern. Instrumentalists then echo play and sing the new pattern.
10. Have all rotate to a new position (singers to instruments and visa versa), and play the game again and again.

Snowflakes

By CRISTI CARY MILLER
and KATHLYN REYNOLDS

LESSON PLAN SNOWFLAKES

TEACHING SUGGESTIONS

1. Sing the song for the students, snapping on the rests. Ask them what the snaps represent and where they occur.
2. Echo-teach the song (with snaps) using two-measure phrases. Then internalize the snaps and sing until learned.
3. Add choreography and sing again.

RHYTHM IDEA

To prepare: *Make eight snowflakes (laminated and transferable). Place one on each line of the following chart:*

1. Display chart. Point to each snowflake and have the students say "snow" (or a one-syllable word of your choice). Relate that each icon is a beat.
2. Give several students the chance to point and lead the others. To reinforce steady beat, play the piano introduction while they perform this task.
3. Randomly remove a snowflake from the chart and explain the empty space represents a silence (or a rest.) Practice speaking the new snowflake pattern.
4. Continue creating different snowflake rhythms to perform with the piano interlude.

EXTENSION IDEA

1. Choose one student to create a rhythm by removing a snowflake(s) from the chart.
2. Sing the song together. As the piano interlude is played, this student points and leads the class to perform his/her pattern.
3. As the song is sung again, the first student chooses another one to make up a new rhythm. This student then becomes the new leader.
4. Continue this process until all have had an opportunity to participate.

There's a Little Wheel a-Turnin'

Traditional
**Arranged by CRISTI CARY MILLER
and KATHLYN REYNOLDS**

heart,_____ in my heart._____There's a lit-tle wheel_ a-turn-in' in my heart.
heart,_____ in my heart._____There's a lit-tle beat_ a-beat-in' in my heart.
heart,_____ in my heart._____There's a lit-tle song_ a-sing-in' in my heart.

LESSON PLAN TEACHING SUGGESTIONS

1. Sing all three verses for the students. Have them place their hands on their heart every time they hear the word "heart."

2. Ask them to recall the verses in sequential order. Write the main idea for each one on the board.

3. With the students, explore movement suggestions to match each verse. Perform the song together with the new actions.

ORFF TEACHING SUGGESTIONS

Have students:

1. Pat the BX crossover pattern while singing the words "crossing over." Transfer to instruments and play while singing the first verse/chorus.

2. Play the AM pattern in the air, alternating hands for each note. Transfer to instrument and play against the BX part while singing the second verse/chorus.

3. Repeat this procedure for the SM part. Transfer and sing the third verse/chorus.

4. Snap the AG/SG pattern while speaking the "think" words. Demonstrate how this part interacts with the lyrics. Transfer to instruments and play in ensemble while singing the song.

MOVEMENT SUGGESTIONS

Formation: *Small groups of four, making small circles/wheels*

VERSE 1
MS. 1-8   Walk CW with R palms down and extended to center, stacked together
MS. 9-10   Pat, clap, tap hands of partners to each side (Repeat)

VERSE 2
MS. 1-8   Walk CCW and extend L palms
MS. 9-10   Pat, clap, tap hands of partners to each side (Repeat)

VERSE 3
MS. 1-8   Walk CW and extend R palms
MS. 9-10   Pat, clap, tap hands of partners to each side (Repeat)

Fairly Renaissance

By CRISTI CARY MILLER
and KATHLYN REYNOLDS

9

LESSON PLAN FAIRLY RENAISSANCE

ORFF TEACHING SUGGESTIONS

To prepare: *On a visual, write out each instrumental melody separately, using different colored markers to denote each part, i.e. BX/BM in red, AX/SX in blue, etc. Label the A and B sections. Write the letter names under all notes.*

1. BX/BM: Remove the E and B bars from the D to D' octave scale.

   a. Display the BX/BM part. As you point to the notes, have students echo-sing each four-measure phrase with note names.

   b. Repeat echo process while pretending to play the music in the "air."

   c. When both A and B section parts are secure, transfer to instruments. Allow time for your instrumentalists to discover this melody on their instrument and practice it.

2. AM: Remove B and C bars from the D to D' octave scale and replace with B♭ and C#.

   a. Divide into two parts, upper and lower melodies. Teach each part separately.

   b. Follow the BX/BM procedure. (Both melodies can be played on the same instrument by two students.)

3. AX/SX: Remove the C' bar and replace with C#'. Follow the BX/BM procedure.

4. AG/SG: Remove E, B, F' and G' bars. Follow the BX/BM procedure.

5. RECORDER: Plays for A section only
Allow time for players to refresh learned notes and practice part.

6. HAND DRUM/TAMBOURINE: Plays for A section only
Teach parts as one pattern, having students clap the hand drum ostinato and snap the tambourine part. Transfer to instruments.

7. Practice in ensemble until perfected and ready to accompany the dance.

MOVEMENT IDEA

Formation: *Concentric circles, with the inside group facing a partner in the outside circle*

1. Partners place their right hands together, shoulder high and palms flat, and place their left hands behind their backs.

2. **A SECTION**
  MS. 1-4:   Step forward-close/step back-close (two times).
  MS. 5-8:   Walk in a clockwise circle with partners, palms still touching.
  On repeat, use left hands and walk counterclockwise.

3. **B SECTION**
  MS. 9-10:   Release hands and step-close to the right, ending with a bow/curtsey.
  MS. 11-12: Step-close to the left, ending with a bow/curtsey.
  MS. 13-16: Circle around partners without turning around and return "home" (a la "do-si-do") with hands behind back.

4. **A SECTION**
Repeat the above A section. End by sliding to the right and face a new partner on the last measure.

5. **INTERLUDE:** With new partner, stand ready to perform dance again.

PERFORMANCE SUGGESTION

Create your own May Day Celebration, a la "Renaissance Fair."
Add this poem as an overture to open the festivities:

> ### "MAY BREEZES"
> ANONYMOUS
>
> *When May breezes melt all the snow from the trees,*
> *The tiny blue violets look up thro' the leaves.*
> *And the birds who have slept thro' the long winter night,*
> *Awaken and greet thee with joy and delight.*
> *Awaken and greet thee with joy and delight.*

- Poem
- Introduction: Instrumentals play first four measures
- Dance with instrumental accompaniment.
- Interlude: First four measures
- Repeat dance with accompaniment several times.

Follow the Drinkin' Gourd

African-American Spiritual
Arranged by CRISTI CARY MILLER and KATHLYN REYNOLDS

* You may choose to find and sing the additional verses.

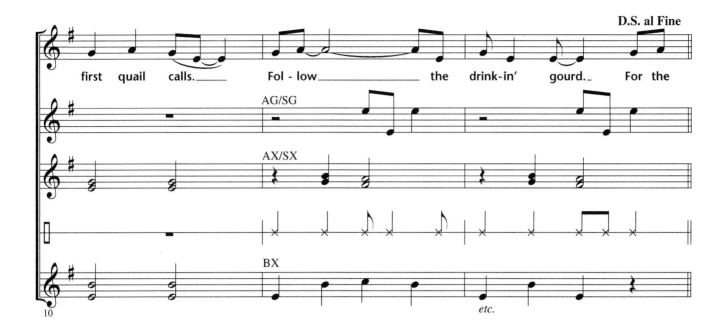

first   quail   calls.____   Fol - low_____   the   drink-in'   gourd._   For the

AG/SG

AX/SX

BX

etc.

10

LESSON PLAN TEACHING SUGGESTIONS

1. To introduce this song, take time to discuss its story and historical background. (A spiritual with instructions embedded in the words to follow the drinking gourd or "Big Dipper." The handle of this constellation points to the North Star that helped guide the slaves to freedom.)

2. Use a copy of the song to give your students the opportunity to discover and review music signs and symbols found there.

3. Sing the melody on "loo" as students follow the melodic line. Stop randomly and ask them to identify the word on which you stopped. Repeat process several times.

4. Add the words (remember, other verses are available) and sing until secure.

ORFF TEACHING SUGGESTIONS

1. Alternately pat the BX pattern using a crossover motion while speaking the "think" words. Explain they will play this pattern for the entire song except during the verse section (ms. 9-12). Transfer to instrument.

2. Play the AX/SX pattern in the air using "think" words and moving hands to show pitch changes. Transfer to instruments and point out changed pattern in the final measure (m. 8). Play against the BX part while singing.

3. Alternately snap the AG/SG ostinato while speaking the "think" words. Transfer to instruments, again noting changed pattern in final measure.

4. Add the metallophone part to the verse measures and include in ensemble.

5. Clap the hand drum ostinato while speaking the "think" words. Transfer to instrument(s).

6. Sing and play together.

Fun wa ni alaafia

Yoruba Welcome Song
Arranged by CRISTI CARY MILLER
and KATHLYN REYNOLDS

Think: "Wel-come to one and all"

5

LESSON PLAN FUN WA NI ALAAFIA

TEACHING SUGGESTIONS

To prepare: *Create a visual of the "voice" part.*

1. Review "syn-co-pa" rhythms with your students.
   Have them find these patterns in the song and rhythm read the song together.

2. To help establish the pitches of this melody, use a pentatonic tone ladder.
   Have students sing echoes of patterns you point to and sing with solfege names.

3. Without singing, use the ladder and point to the pitches in rhythm of the A
   section, one measure at a time, and challenge the students to sing back in solfege.

4. Continue this process using two measures, then entire song.

5. Have students look at the visual and together label the solfege pitches.
   Now sing in rhythm with solfege.

6. Transfer to words and sing again.

7. Speak through the B section together in rhythm.

ORFF TEACHING SUGGESTIONS

1. Have students pat the BX pattern, moving hands to show pitch directions.
   Transfer to instrument.

2. Ask students to practice the AX crossover pattern, tapping knees with fingers.
   Transfer to instrument and play against the BX ostinato.

3. Play again to accompany the song.

UNPITCHED PERCUSSION TEACHING SUGGESTIONS

1. Choose a student who has strong steady beat skills to perform the cowbell part.

2. As the cowbell is being played, perform the Conga drum pattern for the class several times.

3. Ask the students to pat this pattern on their legs with you.
   When they are confident, transfer a student to the instrument.

4. Continue adding the djembe, shakera, and guiro using this process. Practice all together.

5. Add this percussion accompaniment to the Orff patterns and play again, singing the song.

6. Teach the B section rhythm using "think" words. Add to the spoken part and perform.

MOVEMENT IDEA

Formation: *2 lines facing each other*

A SECTION

MS. 1 – 2:	Step-close to R (4 times) followed by a clap on the rest
MS. 3 – 4:	Step-close to L (4 times) followed by a clap on the rest (Repeat)

B SECTION

MS. 5:	Swing R hand out to side and up to shoulder level, palms facing outward
MS. 6:	Hold position
MS. 7:	Repeat with L hand
MS. 8:	Clap partners hands on "Oh" and clap own hands on "yes" (Repeat)

Jump Jive

By CRISTI CARY MILLER
and KATHLYN REYNOLDS

LESSON PLAN JUMP JIVE

TEACHING SUGGESTIONS

To prepare: *Create a visual of phrases 1, 2, and 4 found in the A Section; use different colors for presentation. Place these on a board in random order.*

A SECTION

1. Sing melody on "doo" as students observe visuals. Challenge them to identify the melodic order.

2. Add words and have them echo sing each phrase. Continue until song is learned.

3. To reinforce rhythm-reading skills, ask students to locate the syncopated patterns.

B SECTION

1. Have students echo clap and speak the repeated phrase.

2. Ask them to find a partner and practice the following hand jive pattern:

BEAT 1: With R palms together; slap L palms above

BEAT 2: Slap L palms below

BEAT 3: Keep L palms together; slap R palms below

BEAT 4: Slap R palms above

BEATS 5-8: Repeat the above 4 steps

BEATS 9-10: Tap R elbows (2 times)

BEATS 11-12: Tap L elbows (2 times)

BEATS 13-16: Tap sides of both fists (4 times)

OSTINATO TEACHING SUGGESTIONS

To prepare: *Create a visual of the patterns with "think" words.*

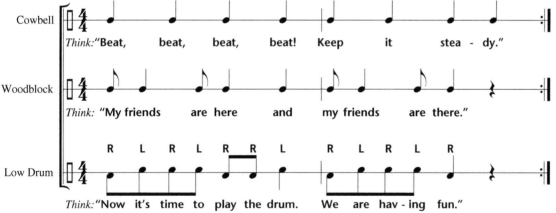

Cowbell — Think: "Beat, beat, beat, beat! Keep it stea - dy."

Woodblock — Think: "My friends are here and my friends are there."

Low Drum — Think: "Now it's time to play the drum. We are hav - ing fun."

1. CLAP the cowbell part while speaking the "think" words. Transfer and play.

2. Alternately SNAP the woodblock pattern (with "think" words). Transfer and play against the cowbell part.

3. PAT the low drum ostinato (with "think" words). Transfer and play against other parts.

4. Perform in ensemble while singing the A section melody.

In Conclusion

• Have students sing as they walk randomly around the room (with instrumental and piano accompaniment).

• At the end of the A section, students find a partner and perform the hand jive with spoken greeting.

Let us Give Thanks

O WALY WALY, English Folksong
Arranged with New Words by CRISTI CARY MILLER
and KATHLYN REYNOLDS

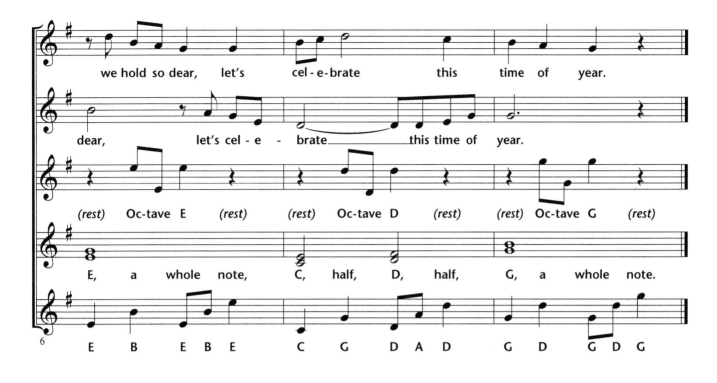

we hold so dear,	let's	cel-e-brate	this	time of	year.

dear,	let's cel-e-brate	this time of	year.

| (rest) | Oc-tave E | (rest) | (rest) | Oc-tave D | (rest) | (rest) | Oc-tave G | (rest) |

| E, | a | whole | note, | C, | half, | D, | half, | G, | a | whole | note. |

| E | B | E | B | E | C | G | D | A | D | G | D | G | D | G |

LESSON PLAN TEACHING SUGGESTIONS

To prepare: *Make a visual of the melody. Also, make a visual of the four descant countermelody phrases (no words), each a different color.*

1. Sing the song for the class to establish the melodic line.

2. Sing again, having the group echo each phrase.

3. To teach the countermelody, have the children listen as you sing each phrase on "loo." Hold up your fingers to denote which phrase you are singing and ask if any phrases are the same. (No)

4. Ask the class to look at the four color-coded phrases as you repeat this process. Challenge the students to place these phrases in sequential order. (Hint: Have them discover one phrase at a time.)

5. Finally, let the class see the visual of the song. Have the students sing through each part.

6. When students are able to sing both parts confidently, divide into two groups and sing together. Switch parts and sing again.

ORFF TEACHING SUGGESTIONS

To prepare: *Download the "paper xylophone" found on the Music Express website – www.musicexpressmagazine.com – Teachers' Corner, Extension Activities. Make a copy for each student.*

Have students:

1. Pat the BX/AX crossover pattern until muscle memory is secure.

2. Look at their paper xylophones and ask them to practice this motion with each symbol (i.e. circles, squares, stars). Circles show the G-D pattern in M. 1. Squares show the E-B pattern in M. 3. Stars show the C-G-D-A-D pattern in M. 4.

3. Transfer to instruments and practice, practice, practice!

4. Speak the "think" words for the AM/SM pattern while pretending to play this part in the air. To simplify, have students learn the bottom note first and then add the note above. Transfer to instruments and play against the BX/AX part.

5. Snap the AG/SG part in rhythm while speaking the "think" words. Transfer to instruments and play in ensemble.

Let's Go to Mexico

By CRISTI CARY MILLER
and KATHLYN REYNOLDS

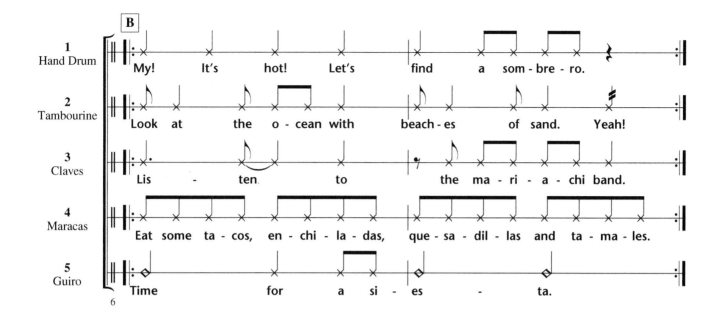

LESSON PLAN TEACHING SUGGESTIONS

1. To set the mood for this spirited music activity, teach the spoken ostinati with the body percussion shown below; practice until secure:

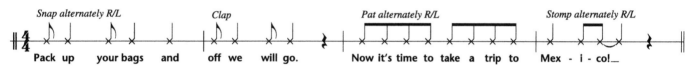

2. To teach the A section, clap the rhythm of the first four measures while speaking the rhythm syllables, stopping after each measure. Ask students to recognize same/different measures.

3. Have them echo back each measure with rhythm syllables. Add words and speak/clap again.

4. Sing the melody on "loo," one measure at a time, and as students echo back, have them draw the melodic direction in the air.

5. Add the words to the melody and practice until learned.

6. To teach the B section, create a visual of each rhythm with words.

7. Teach the patterns one at a time by speaking/clapping the words in rhythm.

8. After each pattern is learned, transfer to suggested instrument.

9. When all ostinati are proficient, practice layering in one at a time beginning with the top pattern.

ORFF TEACHING SUGGESTIONS

To prepare: *Create a visual of the Orff parts.*

1. BX pattern: Have students mallet this part in the air while speaking the "think" words. Transfer to instrument.

2. AX pattern: Ask students to clap this rhythm while speaking the "think" words. Transfer to instrument and play against the BX part.

3. SX pattern: Repeat above procedure.

4. AG/SG pattern: Alternately snap the ostinato while speaking the "think" words. Transfer to instrument.

5. Add the maracas and play in ensemble.

SUGGESTED FORM

- **INTRO:** Spoken ostinati with body percussion
- **A SECTION:** Layer in Orff, one pattern (4 m.) at a time, beginning with BX, then AX/SX, then AG/SG
- Add melody and sing/play in ensemble
- **B SECTION:** Ostinato #1 (w/repeat)
- **A SECTION:** Repeat above without Orff layering
- **B SECTION:** Ostinato #2, then adding Ostinato #1
- **A SECTION**
- **B SECTION:** Ostinato #3, layering in #2, then #1

Continue until all ostinati have been introduced, finishing with the A section.

Let's Take a Walk

"White Coral Bells"
Arranged With New Words by
CRISTI CARY MILLER and KATHLYN REYNOLDS

Voices: Let's take a walk up-on a win-t'ry day.

AG/SG: *Think:* "Guide our way."

AM/SM: *Think:* "E C A G

BX/AX: *Think:* "Walk - ing, walk - ing move a - long."

Voices: All the Christ-mas* lights will help to guide our way. Oh, don't you hear our

E C D G E"

Voices: mer - ry Christ-mas* song. Join our hap-py voi-ces as we move a - long.

LESSON PLAN LET'S TAKE A WALK

TEACHING SUGGESTIONS

1. Give each student a pencil and an 8 ½" x 11" blank piece of paper folded in half lengthwise.

2. Have them listen as you play the entire melody on the piano. (Some students may recognize this song as "White Coral Bells.")

3. Now explain that they will be listening again and drawing a sound map of the song's melodic contour on their papers. (This image will visually show the up, down and repeated tones.)

4. Play the first two phrases of the song as the students listen and draw a sound map on the top half of the folded paper.

5. Have students turn their papers over and play the last two phrases of the song, having them draw again.

6. Ask students to unfold their papers and tell about their discoveries.
   (The top half should look similar to the bottom half denoting like phrases.)

7. Teach the melody and words and practice until secure.

8. Divide the class into two groups and perform as a round. Switch parts and sing again.

ORFF TEACHING SUGGESTIONS

To prepare: *Create a two-measure visual of the BX/AX and AG/SG ostinati. For AM/SM, the visual should show all four measures.*

1. Have students follow the BX/AX visual and alternately pat this part while speaking the "think" words. Transfer to instruments and play as everyone sings.

2. Have students snap the AG/SG part while following the visual and speaking the "think" words. Transfer to instruments and play against the BX/AX part.

3. Teach the AM/SM pattern two measures at a time following the visual. Ask students to play the pattern in the air as they speak the "think" letters. Transfer to instruments and play in ensemble as everyone sings.

MOVEMENT IDEA

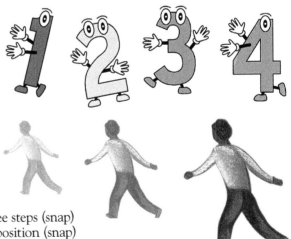

Formation: *Square with four equal lines facing center; Number off lines 1, 2, 3, 4.*

1. Teach this walking pattern to accompany each phrase.
   (Teach lines separately!)

   PHRASE 1: Walk forward three steps and snap on beat 4
   Walk backward three steps and snap on beat 4

   PHRASE 2: Walk backward three steps (snap)
   Walk forward three steps (snap)

   PHRASE 3: (¼ turn to R) Walk forward three steps (snap)
   Walk backward three steps (snap)

   PHRASE 4: (¼ turn center) Make half CW turn in place on three steps (snap)
   Continue half CW turn three steps round to home position (snap)

2. To perform as a two-part round, lines 1 and 3 sing together and begin first. Lines 2 and 4 enter second with singing and movement.

3. Extend this movement idea into a four-part round (with each line singing and moving independently) to songs such as "Christmas Is Coming." Or, consider using this four-line movement as you walk to these instrumental compositions: "Sleigh Ride" or "Overture" from *The Nutcracker Suite*.

Long May Your Colors Wave

By CRISTI CARY MILLER
and KATHLYN REYNOLDS

Vs. 1 Present R hand L to R
Vs. 2 Hands on hips

Present L hand R to L
Present hands

Look - ing a - cross the U. S. A. we hon - or this won - drous
proud to be called A - mer - i - cans; be - side her we'll al - ways

land. We're stand.

Place R hand across heart

We pledge al - le - giance

to this na - tion, land of the free and brave. A -

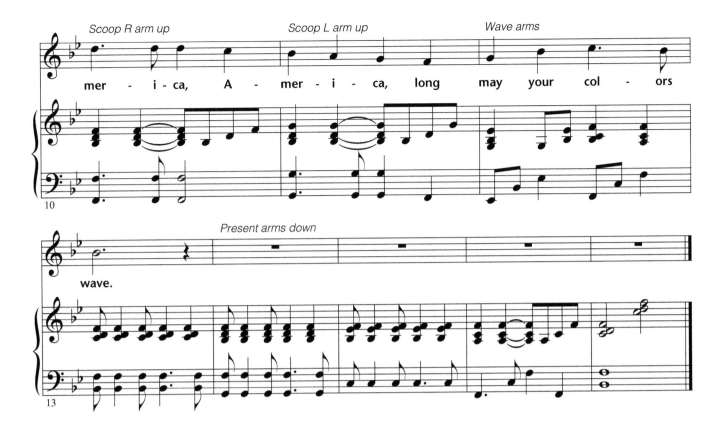

Scoop R arm up ... *Scoop L arm up* ... *Wave arms*

mer - i - ca, A - mer - i - ca, long may your col - ors

Present arms down

wave.

LESSON PLAN TEACHING SUGGESTIONS

To prepare: *Create a visual of the song and choral reading for every student.*

CHORAL READING

*We're proud to live in this great land
That our brave forefathers found.
With lakes and plains and mountains grand,
There's beauty all around.*

*We fought for our independence;
George Washington led the way.
And the writers of the Constitution
Gave us laws we must obey.*

*Many presidents served our nation.
Abraham Lincoln would hear the call
To give to us a proclamation.
Freedom's bell would ring for all.*

*America, we now salute you
With a motto we'll uphold.
A government "of the people, by the people,
for the people."
A democratic nation to behold.*

1. Ask your students to locate measures from the melodic staff of the song that contain: syncopation, descending quarter notes, half/dotted half notes, whole rests, etc.

2. Review or teach the music "road signs," i.e. repeats, 1st/2nd endings.

3. Introduce the melody on the piano. Have students finger point the notes as you play.

4. After students have heard the melody several times, have them join you in singing. Practice until secure.

5. Add the suggested choreography and sing again.

6. Read through the choral reading together and discuss the persons/historical facts found there.

7. Perform again and encourage expressive speaking.

SUGGESTED FORM FOR PRESENTATION

- **INTRODUCTION** (piano plays mm. 13-16)
- **SONG WITH CHOREOGRAPHY** (piano plays all except m. 17)
- **CHORAL READING – VS. 1** (piano plays mm. 13-16 to accompany)
- **SONG WITH CHOREOGRAPHY** (piano plays all except m. 17)
- **CHORAL READING – VS. 2** (piano plays mm. 13-16 to accompany)

Continue process, ending with song.

Music Brings Us All Together

1st time - Part I only
2nd time - Part I & II
3rd time - Part I, II & III

By CRISTI CARY MILLER
and KATHLYN REYNOLDS

Part I — Wave arms: R L R L   Sunburst hands out and down
Mu - sic brings us all to - geth - er. Songs to sing so hap - pi - ly.

Part II — Raise R arm low to high w/ palm up   Lower R arm
Friends, friends are made when we are sing - ing.

Part III — Pat Clap Pat Clap Roll arms low to high Shrug R Shrug L Point to audience Point to self
Mu - sic has a rhy - thm and a me - lo - dy. Ly - rics tell a sto - ry for you_ and_ me.

Present hand out and down   Hook elbows w/ neighbors Plié Up
Mu - sic is the com - mon lan - guage as we blend in har - mo - ny.

Raise L arm low to high with palm up   Lower L arm
Join, join a - long and soon you will a - gree.

Pat Clap Pat Clap Roll arms low to high   Shrug R Shrug L Present high R Present high L
Sing a hap - py tune then sing a - long the way. When I sing a song it makes my day.

LESSON PLAN MUSIC BRINGS US ALL TOGETHER

TEACHING SUGGESTIONS

To prepare: *Create a visual of the song.*

1. Sing one of the three melodies on "loo" and challenge the children to discover which
was performed. Continue this process for the remaining tunes.

2. Now, take your students on a Musical Seek-n-Find by asking questions about the three melodies.
For example, "Which melody primarily uses half notes, (quarter notes, eighth notes)?"
"Where do you find ascending (descending) melodic patterns?" "If 'Do' is 'F', on which solfege pitch
does Part I (Part II, Part III) begin?" "How many quarter notes do you find in all three melodies?"

3. Play the Part I melody on a keyboard. At random, stop on a note and have the children identify
the word connected to the pitch. Do this many times in order for them to internalize the melody.
Add the words and sing together, adding the suggested choreography.

4. Teach Part II by singing the melody *a cappella*. Have the students listen and move their hands
to match the pitch direction. Add the words and sing together, adding the suggested choreography.

5. Sing Part III on "loo," holding up fingers to identify each 2-measure phrase.
Ask the students to identify like phrases.

6. Teach phrases 1 & 3 with words by rote. Have the students sing these phrases while you sing phrases
2 & 4. Switch parts and perform again. Now, sing all together, adding the suggested choreography.

8. Divide your singers into three groups and assign a melody/movement to each one. Have Part I sing
their tune alone. Have them repeat, adding Part II. Finally, layer in Part III as the students perform
the three melodies in harmonic ensemble.

9. Reassign parts and present again until all have experienced each melody. Include the Orff instrumental
ostinati as an accompaniment.

ORFF TEACHING SUGGESTIONS

To prepare: *Create a visual of the following Orff patterns.*

Using the visual, have the students clap the rhythm of the ostinati while speaking rhythm syllables.

Place partners on instruments and ask them to isolate the bars needed for their pattern.

Guide each group in playing their ostinato.

Practice playing each pattern while singing the corresponding melody.

Music Makes Me Move

By CRISTI CARY MILLER
and KATHLYN REYNOLDS

LESSON PLAN MUSIC MAKES ME MOVE

TEACHING SUGGESTIONS

Form a large standing circle to teach the following.
Speak the song in rhythm for the class to hear.

1. Ask students to echo speak the lyrics in rhythm using two-measure phrases, then four-measure phrases. Finally, rhythm-speak the entire song together.

2. Next, teach the actions to the song as you rhythm-speak the words using the above procedure. (Have students perform actions with imaginary partners.)

3. When actions and words are secure, add the melody, one phrase at a time.

4. Practice the song/actions together several times.

5. Now form concentric circles – inside circle facing outward.

6. Perform song and movement with a partner in the opposite circle. On the last phrase, hop to the right to a new partner and continue until all are back to original position.

ORFF TEACHING SUGGESTIONS

Have students:

1. Watch as you play the BX part on the instrument while you sing the "think" words.

2. Pretend to play this ostinato in the air while they sing the "think" words. Transfer to instrument.

3. Repeat the above procedure for the AX/SX pattern. Transfer to instrument and play against the BX part.

4. Clap the AG/SG ostinato while singing the "think" words. (Encourage students to pump hands outward to feel the rests.) Transfer to instruments.

5. Spend time learning the ostinati change for the last measure.

6. Practice until secure, and finally play together in ensemble to accompany the song.

One Wintry Night

**By CRISTI CARY MILLER
and KATHLYN REYNOLDS**

Descant

4. Stars came out one

Voices

1., 4. The stars came out one win - try night. The
2. A song came out one win - try night. Its
3. Joy was felt one win - try night. 'Twas

AG/SG

Think: "Stars came out on a win - try night"

SX/SM

AX/AM

BX/BM

Think: "D   A   A   D   A"

win - try   night.   Stars   came

air   was   crisp_____ and   cold.   The stars came out one
sound   was   loud_____ and   clear.   A song came out one
sent   down   from_____ a - bove.   Joy was felt one

5

word markings on staff:

out | one | win - try | night.

win - try | night. | The | whole | world | to___ | be - | hold.
win - try | night. | for | all | the | world___ | to | hear.
win - try | night. | The | world | was | filled___ | with | love.

8

* Stop on last time

LESSON PLAN TEACHING SUGGESTIONS

To prepare: *Make a copy of the song (including Orff) for each student.*

1. Read the lyrics as a poem to the students and together take time to discuss any feelings evoked from the words.
2. Give each student a copy of the song and have them locate the "poem."
3. Explain that this staff is the vocal line. Ask them to listen and follow as you play it on a piano.
4. Play again, randomly stopping throughout. Challenge students to identify the word connected to the pitch. Continue this game until the melody has been heard many times.
5. Invite the students to join you in singing the song.
6. Ask students to look at the staff labeled descant. Initiate a discussion about the rhythm and melodic direction of this part as compared to the other vocal line.
7. Sing the descant. Have students listen and move their hands to match the melodic direction. Then ask them to sing with you as they continue moving their hands.
8. Divide the class into two groups. Have all sing verses 1-3 together. On verse 4, one group sings the vocal line while the other sings the descant. Switch parts and perform again.

ORFF TEACHING SUGGESTIONS

1. Have students look at the Orff patterns found in the music. Lead them to recognize each ostinato is a repetitive phrase.
2. BX/BM: Alternately pat the pattern while speaking the "think" words. Transfer to instruments and play.
3. AX/AM & SX/SM: Pat the ostinato, moving hands R/L to denote pitch change. Transfer to instruments and play against the BX/BM part.
4. AG/SG: Play this part in the air while speaking the "think" words. Transfer to instruments and play against the other ostinati.
5. Play in ensemble while singing the song.

Suggested Form for Presentation

- **1ST VERSE**: Vocal line accompanied by AX/AM & SX/SM
- **2ND VERSE**: Add BX/BM
- **3RD VERSE**: Add AG/SG
- **4TH VERSE**: Add descant

Pass the Rock

By CRISTI CARY MILLER
and KATHLYN REYNOLDS

Voices — Pass the rock a-round the cir-cle. Keep it hid-den, not to show.

Glockenspiels — *Think:* "Oc-tave jump! Oc-tave jump a-gain!"

Metallophones

Tambourine — *Think:* "a-round, rock"

Hand Drum — *Think:* "Let's pass the rock. Let's pass the rock."

Xylophones — *Think:* "E! B! Cross-ing o-ver. E! B! Cross and stop."

Pass the rock a-round the cir-cle. If you're caught, then in you go.

etc.

5 *etc.*

LESSON PLAN PASS THE ROCK

TEACHING SUGGESTIONS

1. Begin with a discussion of major/minor tonalities.
Explain that major chords/songs have a brighter color whereas minor ones are darker sounding.

2. Have students listen as you play a C major chord followed by a C minor chord.
Let them hear how the third tone is altered to make the chords different.

3. Play major or minor chords on the piano and have students decide if they are "bright yellow" (major) or "dark blue" (minor). Be sure to play these chords at various pitch levels.

4. Now, sing the song (or play on the piano) and have students decide whether it is major or minor.

5. Teach the song by rote and practice until learned.

ORFF TEACHING SUGGESTIONS

1. Have students alternately pat the xylophone ostinato using the "think" words.
Transfer to instruments and play while singing the song.

2. Ask students to play metallophone part in the air, moving hands to show pitch direction.
Transfer to instruments and play against the xylophones as all sing.

3. Have students alternately snap the glockenspiel pattern while speaking the "think" words.
Transfer to instruments and play against the xylophone and metallophone ostinati.

4. Teach the hand drum and tambourine part as one ostinato, patting the hand drum pattern and clapping the tambourine part. Transfer to instruments and play in ensemble with Orff instruments as everyone sings song.

PASSING GAME

Formation: *Seated circle*

1. Student's left palm faces up and is cupped. The right palm faces down and is fisted.

2. A small rock is passed around the circle as everyone performs this pattern simultaneously:

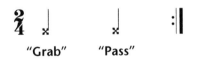

"Grab"   "Pass"

*Grab = right hand picks up rock
(or pretends) from own left palm*
*Pass = right hand passes rock (or pretends)
to person on right's left palm*

3. Add the song to the pattern and practice again.

4. When pattern/song is secure, one person is chosen for the center and closes his/her eyes.
The game begins and on cue from teacher, he/she opens eyes. The object is to keep the rock hidden from this person.

5. The song is repeated continuously until the rock is discovered.
The student caught with the rock then becomes the next center person.

Pretty Little Miss

By CRISTI CARY MILLER and KATHLYN REYNOLDS

Voices

Will you dance with me, my pret-ty lit-tle miss? I'll dance with you, my hon - ey. We'll
Let's swing to the right, my pret-ty lit-tle miss. Let's swing to the left, my hon - ey. Now

AG/SG

Think: "Dance, dance, oh yeah!

SX

Think: "F F C C F F C C

AX

Think: "Round, round com - ing down - ward.

Tambourine (snap)

Hand Drum (clap)

Think: "Dance with me. Dance with me.

Woodblock (pat)

Think: "Pret-ty lit-tle miss, Pret-ty lit-tle miss,

BX/CBB

Think: "Dance, dance, dance, dance, swing.

---

swing a - round and head to town where we'll spend lots of mon - ey.
wave good - bye but keep an eye on the one who's sweet and sun - ny.

Dance, dance, oh yeah!"

F C C C F C G C F F"

Round, round com - ing down."

Dance with me. Dance, dance!"

Yeah!"

Pret-ty lit-tle miss, swing."

Dance, dance, dance, swing, dance."

LESSON PLAN PRETTY LITTLE MISS

TEACHING SUGGESTIONS

Have students:

1. Learn the unpitched instrument ostinato found in the song accompaniment. Substitute the body percussion for the instruments.
2. Perform this ostinato as you sing the melody on "doo." Add the words and perform again.
3. Learn the song by rote and practice together until secure.
4. Divide into two groups, one performing ostinato while the other sings the song. Switch parts and sing again.

PLAY PARTY

Formation: *Concentric circles with partners facing each other, boys on inside/girls on outside*

"Will you dance with me, my pretty little miss?"
    boys bow to girls

"I'll dance with you, my honey."
    girls respond with a curtsey

"We'll swing around and head to town"
    R hands join and boy spins girl CCW

"Where we'll spend lot of money."
    couples promenade CCW

"Let's swing to the right, my pretty little miss."
    Couple R arm swing

"Let's swing to the left, my honey."
    Couple L arm swing

"Now wave goodbye…"
    wave at partner with right hand

"but keep an eye,"
    step touch forward and clap partners hand on "eye"

"On the one who's sweet and sunny."
    step touch backward and then step to their R as you reach to shake new partner's hand on "sunny"

EXTENSION IDEA

To make this a true play party, place one extra boy in the center of the circle.
His goal is to step in and "steal" a girl as the couples are moving to new partners ("sunny.")
The boy who is bumped out becomes the new "eligible bachelor" and takes the center spot.

ORFF SUGGESTIONS

Have students:

1. Pat the BX part while speaking "think" words. Move hands to show chord change. Transfer to instrument.
2. Watch as you play the AX part on a xylophone visual. (Speak the "think" words while demonstrating.) Transfer to instrument and play against the BX part.
3. Pretend to play the SX ostinato in the air while speaking the "think" words. Transfer to instrument.
4. Snap the AG/SG while speaking the "think" words. Transfer to instruments.
5. Add the unpitched instrumental ostinato.
6. Play in ensemble and practice until secure.

The Scene Is Halloween

By CRISTI CARY MILLER
and KATHLYN REYNOLDS

LESSON PLAN THE SCENE IS HALLOWEEN

OSTINATI TEACHING SUGGESTIONS

To prepare: *Create a visual of the following ostinati patterns.*

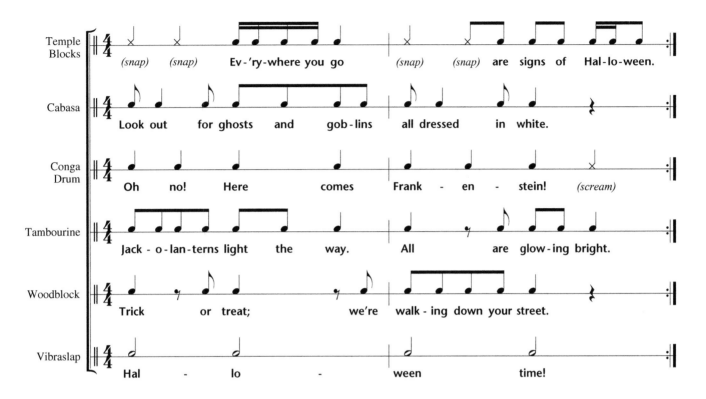

1. Ask for volunteers to individually clap/speak any of the given ostinati. (Applaud the success of those who perform.)

2. After each presentation, have the class respond by performing the pattern.

3. For the more challenging ostinati, clap/speak these parts for them and have them echo back.

4. "Halloween Rhythm Charade" – When all are secure with each ostinato, play this game. Begin by clapping one of the rhythms (without speaking the words) and have students guess the correct one. The student with the correct answer leads the group in performing the ostinato with words. He/she then becomes the next presenter, choosing another pattern. Play the game until all of the ostinati have been discovered many times.

5. Transfer ostinati to suggested instruments. Practice playing each line one at a time. (NOTE: Click mallet sticks together instead of snapping on temple blocks part.)

6. When secure, have students discover layering: begin with the bottom part ("Hal-lo-ween time!") and add on one part at a time. (Layer in as many parts as your group finds successful.)

MELODY / ORFF TEACHING SUGGESTIONS

1. Teach the melody by rote using two-measure phrases. (Snap on the rests to help students feel the "silence.") Sing song until learned.

2. Pat and speak the BX/AX pattern to demonstrate the crossover motion. Transfer to instruments and play while singing.

3. Pat the BM/AM part, moving hands to match the pitch changes. Transfer to instruments and play against the BX/AX pattern.

4. Teach the slapstick, guiro and AG/SG patterns together as one ostinato. (Pat = slapstick, clap = guiro and snap = AG/SG.) Perform body percussion pattern while singing the song. Transfer to instruments.

5. Perform all instruments together while singing the song.

Sleigh Ride

By CRISTI CARY MILLER
and KATHLYN REYNOLDS

Voices: Load up the sleigh on this fine day for a jin-gle bell ride. Let's not de-lay. The

AX/SX — *Think:* "F, D, C, B, C, C, C, C,

hors-es trot, their hooves clip clop, as they car-ry us on our way.
in the fun. We've just be-gun on this won-der-ful hol-i-day.

F, D, C, B, C, C, F"

Fine

Gid-dy up! Here we go! Dash-ing through fields of snow. What a great dis-play. Join

D.S. al Fine

LESSON PLAN SLEIGH RIDE

TEACHING SUGGESTIONS

To prepare: *Create a visual for all singers, including the Orff parts.*

1. Review the music road signs (D.S. al Fine) with students, making sure they understand how to read the song.

2. Create a game where you play the melody on a keyboard (or sing on "loo") and randomly stop during the music. Challenge students to identify the word on which you stopped. (Do this process several times.)

3. Next, have them rhythm speak and clap the song. Be certain they are secure with the sixteenth notes before proceeding.

4. Finally, add the melody and words. Have students practice until confident.

ORFF TEACHING SUGGESTIONS

Have students:

1. Alternately pat an eighth note beat while singing the song. Transfer to BX. Add the jingle bell part and perform in tandem.

2. Sing the letter names in pitch for the AX/SX part. Practice again as they pretend to play this pattern in the air. Transfer to instruments and play against the BX/bell parts. (Be aware that these instruments play only ms. 1–4.)

3. Look at ms. 5–6 and identify the SG as the same rhythm pattern as the BX part, only different notes. Transfer to instrument.

4. Pat the AG part while speaking rhythm syllables. Have them move their hands to show pitch change. Transfer to instrument and play against the SG part.

5. Sing the song as instruments accompany.

STICK PASSING GAME

To prepare: *Display the following four-measure rhythm.*

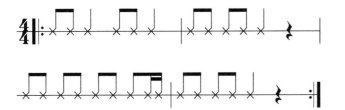

Formation: *Seated circle with each player holding a rhythm stick.*
(There should be an equal number of different colored sticks, e.g. six red sticks, six blue sticks, etc.)
Place a small group of metal instruments, i.e. jingle bells, finger cymbals, triangles, tambourines,
in the circle center, enough to match one set of colored sticks.

1. Review the displayed rhythm as students clap while speaking rhythm syllables. Repeat again as students internalize the syllables.

2. When all are secure, teach the following two-beat stick passing pattern:
   "TOGETHER" = both hands holding stick in center of body
   "PASS" = with R hand, pass stick to player on R while receiving stick in L hand from player on L.
   To successfully perform this pattern, the players need to present palms upward while passing/receiving.

3. Perform the pattern while singing the song. At the conclusion, call out a color and have those students go to the circle center and choose an instrument.

4. Have the class sing as the instrumentalists play the displayed rhythm to accompany the song.

5. Play the game until all have had a chance to accompany.

There's Magic in the Air

By CRISTI CARY MILLER
and KATHLYN REYNOLDS

63

LESSON PLAN THERE'S MAGIC IN THE AIR

TEACHING SUGGESTIONS

To prepare: *Make a visual of the song for all the students to see and read.*

Have students:

1. Echo clap two-measure 6/8 rhythm patterns to experience the feel of this meter.

2. Look at the song visual to discover like rhythm patterns.

3. Learn the A section as they follow the visual. Ask them to echo speak/clap the song lyrics/rhythm in two-measure phrases.

4. Echo sing in two-measure phrases. Extend to four-measure phrases and sing until learned.

5. Learn the B section by following a solfege step ladder. Point to the pitches and sing the solfege in two-measure phrases as students echo.

6. Repeat process with lyrics and sing until secure.

7. Follow the visual as they sing all of the song.

ORFF TEACHING SUGGESTIONS

To prepare: *Write each instrumental accompaniment on giant staff paper. Use a different color to represent each part. (Put the unpitched instruments together.)*

A SECTION

Hint: *This 11-measure Orff accompaniment is in 4-3-4 form with the first/last four measures the same and the middle three different.*

Have students:

1. Alternately pat the first four measures of the BX part while speaking the "think" words. Point out this pattern on the BX visual. Speak the letter names ("think" words) of the next three measures while pretending to play these notes in the air. Put all together and transfer to instruments.

2. Clap the first four measures of the AX part while speaking the "think" words. Follow the above process and transfer to instruments.

3. Follow the visual while snapping the AG part and speaking the "think" words. Transfer to instrument.

4. Add the unpitched percussion and practice playing together.

B SECTION

Have students:

1. Pat the AM/BM part as they follow the visual, speaking the "think" words. Transfer to instruments and play until secure.

2. Pretend to the play the SX part in the air as they follow the visual and speak the "think" words. Transfer to instrument and play against the AM/BM pattern.

3. Again, pretend to the play the SG part in the air as they follow the visual and speak the "think" words. Encourage them to use a crossover for this pattern. Transfer to instrument and play all instruments together.